Photographs by:
Frank Naylor
M Gilroy

Front cover painting by:
D A Lish

**The publishers would like to thank Paul and Sue Field of Fur
Feather 'n' Fins, Lewes, for allowing photographs to be taken of
their stock.**

Your First
CHIPMUNK

INTRODUCTION

Most people recognise the chipmunk from the dark stripes running down its back.

WHAT IS A CHIPMUNK?

There are approximately 40 species and sub-species of chipmunk. When they first started being kept as pets in the 1950s, most chipmunks came from the genus *Tamias striatus*, which lives in the forests of Eastern Canada and North America. However, more often than not, chipmunks kept in captivity today come from the genus *Eutamias*, whose territory ranges over Western and North America, Canada, Mexico, Siberia, Mongolia, China and Korea. It is very likely that your first chipmunk will be the relatively large Siberian chipmunk, *Eutamias sibericus*.

The average European and Asian chipmunk weighs about 100–125g (3.5–4.4oz). Its body is about 8–16cm (3–6in) long and its bushy tail adds another 6–14cm (2.3–5.5in). It is an attractive little animal, with distinctive dark stripes running down the sandy-coloured back and along the tail.

The Eastern American species is larger, with a body length of 13–18cm (5–7in), and a reddish-brown tail of 7–13cm (2.7–5.1in). The fur on the back is reddish-brown, and the dark stripes alternate with grey or brown. The belly fur is white or off-white and the hindquarters are quite red.

CHIPMUNK BEHAVIOUR

If you understand a little of how chipmunks live in the wild, you will be able to care better for your pet at home.

The chipmunk is diurnal, which means that it is awake most of the day and sleeps at night. Some chipmunks can be quite aggressive and, as none of them really like being handled, there is a risk that you will be bitten if you try to pick up your pet. If you want a cuddly pet, the chipmunk is not really suitable but, on the other hand, its lively antics make it an amusing companion.

In the wild, chipmunks live quite solitary lives. They inhabit underground tunnels and burrows which they defend vigorously if the occasion arises. They are active and alert. Being terrestrial (ground dwelling), they are strong burrowers, but they also venture up into the trees to forage for food and therefore are agile climbers. For this reason, your chipmunk should be given as large a cage as possible so that it can exercise. Like hamsters, chipmunks have large internal cheek pouches in which they store food.

In the wild, chipmunks make the most of the warmest parts of the day to feed and play. This means that in the spring you are not likely to see them until mid-morning but, in the summer, they are up and about before dawn. They return to their burrows to rest during the hottest part of the day.

Depending on the climate in their natural habitat, chipmunks hibernate in the winter. In Siberia, for example, they disappear from October until February but in other more temperate parts of the world they will be out and about on mild days.

A chipmunk will collect grass to line its nest.

HANDLING

It may be possible to tame a chipmunk if you get it when it is very young (under four months old) and if you are very gentle. A breeder may have had time to hand-tame the babies but, in any case, if you buy a young chipmunk from a breeder who has tame stock, the baby will be easier to tame.

You must never pick up a chipmunk by the end of its tail. As part of its natural defence mechanism against predators, the loose skin of the tail sheds quite easily. This will be a shock to both you and the animal. However, usually the wound heals quite easily, the dry part drops off and the chipmunk continues with its life not seeming to notice the lack of part of its anatomy. Only hold the tail where it joins the body, and support the body weight with your other hand, with your second and third fingers over the chipmunk's shoulders.

Never chase your pet around its cage as the chipmunk will find this extremely stressful. The best way of catching a chipmunk is to use a lightweight butterfly net. You can gather the chipmunk into the base of the net and bring it up to your chest. (This is the time when you are most likely to get bitten, so you would be wise to invest in a pair of good leather gloves.) Place one hand firmly across the chipmunk's back and support it

If you take lots of care and have lots of patience, your chipmunk may become as tame as this one.

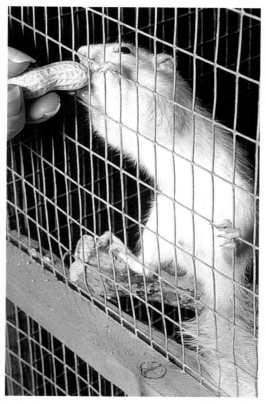

Arm yourself with a tasty treat to tempt your chipmunk to come to the side of the cage. It will soon learn that you bring good things to eat.

from below with your other hand. You can also pick it up with your thumb and forefinger by the thick scruff around its neck, but I would not advise that you do this with a new or untamed animal.

If you want to try to hand tame your chipmunk, you must be very patient and quiet, and you must remember that some chipmunks will never let themselves be handled. If this is the case with yours, respect its wishes.

The process of hand taming is much easier if you have large outdoor housing in which you can sit quietly for some time, but even indoors you should be able to make friends with your pet, although you may get cramp from holding your hand in the cage. Sit quietly and let the animal come to you. Hold a tasty titbit, such as sunflower seeds, peanuts, or raisins. When the chipmunk learns your scent and that you have something nice for it, it may begin to investigate your hand and arm. Eventually, it will take the food from your hand and may even nudge you to stroke it.

As I said previously, the important thing is to be patient. Do not try to pick up the chipmunk before it is ready – if you frighten it, you might undo weeks of patient work.

CHOOSING

First, you should think about why you want to own a chipmunk. Do you want to breed? If so, obviously you will need to get a pair, one of each sex. Do you want just a pet? If so, buy one as young as possible, about 8–16 weeks old, so that you have a better chance of taming it. How much space can you give it? Will it live indoors or out?

Don't forget that your chipmunk might live for four years, or even longer. Some females have been known to live for 12 years. Are you going to be able to look after it properly for that length of time?

When you buy a chipmunk from a pet shop or a breeder, always look for the following signs. The animal should be lively and its coat should have a sheen to it. It should not have any cuts or scars. Make sure its tail is all there. A damaged tail takes away some of the chipmunk's charm and, in addition, it may mean that the animal is older than you think or has been in a fight.

'Bright-eyed and bushy-tailed' certainly describes this happy, healthy chipmunk.

If you want to breed, make sure the two you choose are unrelated, if possible. This lessens the chance of the babies being born with defects or disabilities caused by in-breeding (where the parents are closely related). Also keep this in mind if you go on to breed from the youngsters.

See how the shopkeeper or breeder handles the animals and whether they are being stressed by being caught and handled in the wrong sort of way. It will be more difficult to tame a chipmunk that is even more suspicious than usual of the human race.

As with any small animal, it is important to give your chipmunks as much space as possible. Ideally, a group should be housed outside in a large, high, airy cage like a bird aviary. However, if you do not have this space, or if you want a single chipmunk as a pet indoors, don't worry. A chipmunk can live in a smaller cage.

If you have room, this type of cage is very suitable for the agile, active chipmunk.
Note the two nestboxes, one for each animal.

A pine cone makes a great toy.

INDOOR CAGE

A cage for a chipmunk that is to be kept inside should be at least 90cm high by 45cm wide by 60cm deep (36 x 18 x 24in). There are not many cages made specifically for chipmunks but you can adapt one sold for chinchillas.

First, check that the gap between the wire mesh or bars is no larger than 1cm wide, or your chipmunk will escape. (If you make your own cage, use proper aviary wire as chipmunks can gnaw through chicken netting.)

The cage should be made all of wire, including the floor. Make sure the wire is inside any wooden struts so that the chipmunks cannot get to the wood to gnaw it. Raise the cage on wooden blocks and put a newspaper or litter-lined tray below it. This will allow urine and droppings to fall through to the tray below and make the cage easier to keep clean.

Do add some things for the chipmunk to play on or in. For example, apple and pear branches (well cleaned to prevent infection), rocks, shelves, pipes, thick rope and so on are all good chipmunk toys. Make sure the branches are firmly anchored so that they do not slip around the cage. Do not put in yew, laburnum or rhododendron branches, as these are poisonous.

Provide a sturdy wooden nest box for each animal and hang it on the cage. You could add one or two extra nest boxes in which the chipmunks can store their food. The chipmunks will be less likely to fight if they have plenty of choice. You can hang the box outside the cage and cut a hole in the mesh to allow the chipmunk access. A suitable nest box is one made for a budgerigar.

OUTSIDE CAGE

You can house chipmunks in a shed with an outdoor run or aviary attached. Buy an aviary as big as you can afford, and at least 2m (6.5ft) square, but remember that it will be part of your garden so try to make it look attractive as well. Chipmunks in the wild rarely venture higher than about 2m (6ft) off the ground, so the aviary does not need to be huge. However, consider your own height. It will not be comfortable for you to be cramped in too small an area.

The aviary should have an area that is well sheltered or connected to a shed. I recommend that you use roofing felt rather than corrugated iron or plastic for the roof, as the last two are not such good insulators and the shed is more likely to overheat in summer and be colder in winter. Good ventilation is given by an external wired window, but you must add a shutter that can be raised to different levels to cut out bad weather.

This aviary contains plenty of things for the chipmunk to do.

Hay is an ideal bedding. Put in a good amount and your chipmunks will be warm and cosy, like these Whites.

The base of the cage should be wire, concrete or paving to prevent chipmunks from digging out and other animals from burrowing in. It should be well covered (at least 5–6cm/1.9–2.3in) with peat litter or bark chippings which the chipmunks will dig into and bury their food. Peat is becoming more difficult to find and, in any case, many people involved with conservation feel that it should not be used as it is a non-renewable resource, but there are excellent alternatives on the market.

Again, make the interior interesting for your pets by putting in (well-washed) branches, twigs, logs, pipes and so on. Add one nest box per chipmunk and a couple of spares. It is recommended that these are placed at the same height around the aviary so that the chipmunks do not fight over supposedly preferable positions. Keep them well spaced apart for the same reason.

NESTING MATERIAL

Whether your chipmunks are housed in or out of doors you should provide plenty of nesting material. Meadow hay is particularly good as it absorbs urine and faeces better than wood shavings. However, for an indoor cage which will be cleaned more often, wood shavings are perfectly adequate. Avoid sawdust, as it can irritate the chipmunk's eyes and get into its ears when it burrows.

Do not use man-made fibres and wool as these are very dangerous. Such materials will cause a blockage if the chipmunk eats them, or the fibres can twine around limbs, causing injury.

OTHER EQUIPMENT

Use heavy ceramic food dishes with wide bases so that the chipmunks cannot tip them over easily. It is essential that water is always available. It is best to put it in a glass or plastic water bottle that hangs outside the cage. Chipmunks will gnaw plastic, so a glass bottle is best if it has to hang inside the cage.

CLEANING THE CAGE

Chipmunks are clean animals and use a particular spot in their cage as a toilet. This makes it a fairly simple task to clean the cage. Clean an indoor cage once a week, and a large outdoor cage once a month. As a rule of thumb, if the cage smells, you have left it too long. Remove stale food, but do not throw away every particle as the chipmunks will be alarmed to find their carefully-hoarded store of choice titbits has disappeared.

Both indoor and outdoor cages should be thoroughly scrubbed four times a year with disinfectant. Rinse the cage thoroughly with clean water until the smell has gone.

Clean out the nest boxes – after a litter has been weaned is a good time. Try not to clean them out in winter, as often the chipmunk will hoard seeds in its box.

Always clean food bowls and scrub water bottles each day. Refill the water bottles with fresh water because, although it may not look dirty, the water will become stale.

FEEDING

In the wild, the chipmunk would eat a varied diet of seeds, nuts, berries, shoots from trees and bushes and even eggs, insects, small birds and mice. Therefore, you should try to give a variety of foods to your pet in order to keep it in peak condition.

You can buy a chipmunk and squirrel mix from the pet shop, but this tends to contain a lot of sunflower seeds and peanuts. Chipmunks adore these and will eat them first, then try to persuade you to give them more instead of eating the rest of their food. If you give in, you will soon find that your chipmunks get very fat!

Some fat is needed to keep the animals healthy. You will know if you have been too strict as the chipmunk's coat will look dull. As well as sunflower and peanuts, give walnuts and other hard-shelled nuts such as hazel, almonds and acorns. It will do the chipmunk good to open the shells itself as the gnawing will help to keep its teeth trimmed. Corn is another good addition.

Eggs, especially the whites, are high in protein. Give one raw egg to a pair or group of chipmunks once a week. Another source of protein is worms. Make sure that any worms you dig up from your garden are well washed and do not come from areas where pesticides have been used.

Protein is also available in fruit and vegetables such as bananas, oranges, apples, pears, grapes, bean sprouts, carrots and so on. However, do remove the stones from fruit such as plums and peaches, as they contain a substance which is poisonous to chipmunks. Fruits that contain pips, such as apples, are perfectly all right. Chipmunks will also enjoy small sprigs of fresh garden herbs or flowers such as marigolds and nasturtiums.

Put a cuttlefish bone in the cage. The chipmunks will gnaw on this, which is good for their teeth, and they will obtain calcium from the bone.

Fruit is good for chipmunks because it contains protein, essential for health.

A gourmet selection of food suitable for chipmunks. Do not let your pets gorge themselves on their favourite sunflower seeds or peanuts, or they will get fat.

A chipmunk will eat about 25–30g (0.88–1oz) of food a day, but it likes to have a little left over which it can store. As autumn comes and they prepare for hibernation, put extra food in the cage so that the chipmunks do not fight over it.

If you have a pregnant chipmunk or a mother feeding her young, increase the amount of food offered. When you have had your pets for a while, you will learn how much to give them.

Finally, a word about storage. If you keep the food outside, make sure you store it in airtight and rodent-proof bins. Rats and mice are past masters at sniffing out a free source of food but, if they get into the food, they will contaminate it and disease could be passed on to your chipmunks.

BREEDING

Before you start breeding, first ask yourself what you are going to do with the babies. Will you be able to sell them? Have you room to keep more aviaries or cages to prevent both fighting and in-breeding as the families mature? Genetics is too complicated a subject to cover in this book but, basically, as well as passing on good points, in-breeding can pass on bad ones. You don't want your chipmunks' grandchildren or great-grandchildren to be born with defects.

Next, you have to make sure you have one of each sex. Have a good look at them as they hang onto the wire of the cage. The adult male's penis is visible and, in the breeding season, the scrotum (the sac protecting the testicles) is very enlarged. The distance between the anus and the uro-genital area is greater in males than in females.

Keep breeding pairs, or groups of, for example, one male to 2–3 females. Don't keep more males than females, or they will fight over the females as they come into season.

A female will call from the highest point of the cage.

A female can start to breed in the spring following her birth, and go on until she is six years old. The breeding season extends from March to September, with most activity taking place in April/May and July/August. There are two litters a year, about three months apart.

Top: this is what a male looks like. You can see the genitals quite clearly as he hangs on to the cage.
Below: the male comes to investigate the female's cage.

The female will mate as many times as she can over a 24-hour period.

When the female comes into season she will chirp continuously. You will soon recognise what all the noise is about. For a period of 24 hours she will mate with any male that can catch her. This may cause fighting between the males in groups kept outside. If she is with only one male, she will continue to want to mate even after several meetings, and will flaunt herself in front of him until he gets back his strength and interest. The activity is so intense that, if it went on for more than 24 hours, the poor male would probably collapse!

The length of time a female is pregnant (the gestation period) is usually 31–32 days but it can be slightly less or more. She remains active throughout her pregnancy. There are few signs that she is expecting a litter; in about 10 days her lower mammary glands enlarge slightly and after about 20–25 days the glands further up the body become more noticeable. She begins to look fatter, too.

All through pregnancy, the female will build up her nest box. Give her lots of warm nesting materials to line her nest, and extra food that she can hoard. She needs this as she will not leave her babies for the first 24 hours after they are born.

AFTER THE BIRTH

When the female chipmunk has given birth, do not yield to the temptation to 'have a little look'. If the mother is disturbed, she may abandon her babies, or even kill them. She will eat all the afterbirths (placentas) and any stillborn babies. The placenta contains rich nutrients which help the mother, and also instinctively she wants to remove traces of blood which in the wild would attract predators to the nest.

The young are born naked and blind and are 3cm (1.1in) long. They make a squeaking sound until they are 14 days old but after that they are quite quiet unless they are disturbed.

The mother will come out of her nest when she is sure her young are warm and comfortable and when she is hungry and thirsty. She will not stay out too long as her babies cannot regulate their temperature and get cold easily.

Once the mother starts to return to her normal routine, you can peek into the nest box through the sliding roof or side. Do not disturb the entrance hole as the female blocks it up when she goes out and checks it on her return.

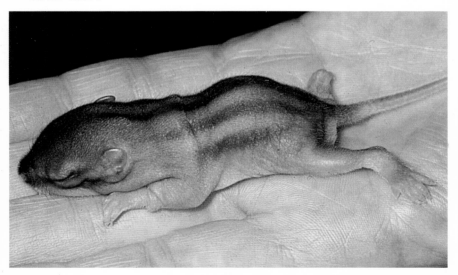

This 8-day-old baby is already showing its dark stripes. Compare its size with the human hand that it is lying on.

Very carefully part the hay until you can see the babies but do not touch them. They will squeak and the mother will hurry back, so be quick. Do not look at them more than once a day and, preferably, only once every two days. Do not invite family, friends and neighbours to view the babies as this is bound to cause them stress.

GROWING UP

The babies' downy coats start to show at about 7 days, and they are fully furred at 16 days. Their eyes open at 26–28 days. They start to venture from the nest at about 35 days, although it can be as early as 30 or as late as 38 – leave it up to them. Give them a platform near the nesting box that they can rest on, and plenty of climbing material. They will learn to forage for food and find the water bottle. Offer the babies small pieces of food such as cereal or oatmeal that they can pick up easily, and add a little dried milk powder to the food which will give the babies extra calcium and vitamin supplementation.

The mother will still suckle the babies (give them milk), but she dries up by the sixth week and then the young are on their own. Do not take the young from her until all the milk has gone, otherwise her mammary glands might become enlarged and painful.

A 36-day old youngster.

THE SECOND LITTER

If the weather conditions are favourable and your female is very fit, she might come into season again later in the year. Generally, second litters are fewer in number and the babies may be smaller in size as the mother may not be in such good condition as earlier in the year. The babies will be born in the autumn, and it is important that there is plenty of warm nest material, as the temperature at night can drop considerably.

It is important to clean out the nest box after the first litter has been weaned so that the female has a clean nursery for the new babies. A dirty box could lead to disease or death among the babies. If she does not become pregnant again, the box will be ready for the winter.

HANDREARING

You may be unlucky enough to lose the mother, or she may abandon her babies. You then have to decide whether or not to rear the young yourself. Handrearing is difficult, time consuming and very tiring. A baby up to the age of three weeks has to be fed every three hours day and night. At four weeks, you can drop the feed between midnight and 6am.

Use the smallest dropper or syringe that you can find at the pharmacy. Feed very slowly, and make sure that no bubbles appear in the nostrils and that the baby does not choke. These are signs that the food is going into the lungs, not the stomach. Hold the baby head-down by its hind legs, supporting the body with a finger, until the lungs are clear. Giving too rich food will give the babies diarrhoea which can easily kill them.

Days 1–7 One part evaporated milk to two parts water with a pinch of glucose.
Days 8–30 Three teaspoons of baby cereal, one teaspoon of evaporated milk, half a teaspoon of honey. Mix with water until it is of a pouring consistency. You can add a vitamin supplement.

After feeding, wipe the babies' mouths with a piece of cotton wool moistened with warm water, and clean around their faces, ears, fur and around their genitalia. It is important to do this last action because, as they have no reflexes to perform these functions themselves, it stimulates the babies to urinate and defecate.

After each feeding session, wash all the equipment you used and sterilize it using the normal sterilizing fluid for human babies. Just before the next feed, rinse the equipment with cool boiled water to remove any unusual taste.

HEALTH

Chipmunks are tough little animals and usually stay healthy as long as they are housed and fed correctly. Problems are usually the result of bad management. Below are some of the commonest ailments but, if you are unsure about your pet's health, do not hesitate to seek advice from your veterinary surgeon.

OVERGROWN INCISORS

A rodent's teeth continue to grow throughout its life, but usually are kept short by the action of gnawing wood and other hard materials. Occasionally the teeth become too long, probably because there is a lack of such gnawing opportunities, or the diet is too soft. You might notice that the fur around the mouth and chin is damp, as though the chipmunk has been dribbling, and perhaps it will only eat soft food. The vet will have to clip or file the teeth, and you will have to ensure that hard materials such as dog biscuits and nuts with hard shells are added to the diet.

Sometimes a front (incisor) tooth is broken as the result of a fall or a fight. In this case, there will be nothing to wear away the opposite tooth of the pair, which may then start to grow too big. The tooth will have to be clipped back until the broken tooth has regrown.

DIARRHOEA

Diarrhoea is when the faeces are very loose and runny. Usually it is caused by too many fresh vegetables. Adjust the diet by adding cornflour or Kaolin to the dried foods until things go back to normal but, if the diarrhoea lasts for more than a couple of days, go to the vet. A small animal like a chipmunk can dehydrate quickly if it is left untreated and may die.

CONSTIPATION

Constipation is the opposite of diarrhoea; in other words, there is a blockage in the intestines. In many cases, this is caused by the chipmunk eating its bedding. Unsuitable bedding material, such as cotton wool or wood waste, will block the intestine. Replace the bedding and give the chipmunk fresh fruit and vegetables. Small pieces of apple and orange are good remedies. If it continues, see the vet.

WOUNDS AND SCRATCHES

Most wounds and scratches are caused by the chipmunk catching itself on a rough piece of wood or metal, or by fighting. A chipmunk's flesh heals very quickly and many minor wounds cause no problems whatsoever. Bathe the wound in a mild antiseptic lotion once a day. If the wound is very deep or becomes infected, you will have to see the vet.

This white chipmunk has lots of space and interesting things to climb on. Gnawing the wood will help to keep her teeth from growing too long.

RESPIRATORY SYSTEM

A chipmunk normally takes 75 breaths a minute. If it has an infection, this rate will first increase and then subside to slower, more laboured breathing. There may not always be a discharge from the nose. The chipmunk could be suffering a disease called Aspergilosis, caused by fungal spores from mouldy or damp hay. Its lungs may have been irritated by tobacco smoke, aerosols, insecticides and so on. Ask your vet about treatment.

Chipmunks can also catch a 'cold' from humans, so if you or any of your family are sniffing and sneezing, try to keep away from your pets. Make sure the cage is in a draught-free area so that the chipmunks do not get chilled.

EYES

A chest infection, draughts or dust or fine sawdust blowing about can cause eye problems. There might be a discharge, or the eyes may appear red and inflamed (conjunctivitis). Wipe away any discharge with a piece of cotton wool soaked in 0.5% saline solution and dry the face gently with a clean piece of cotton wool. If it persists, or the discharge becomes more pus-like, see the vet.

PARASITES

It is very unlikely that your house-bound chipmunk will pick up fleas and lice, but animals kept outside might pick up unwelcome visitors from wild rats or mice.

A skin infection called mange can be caught from infected rodents or domestic pets. Microscopic mites bury into the skin, causing intense itching.

Ringworm, which is a fungal infection, can be contracted from damp, musty bedding, or from contact with infected animals (including man). It causes patchy hair loss with dry, flaky areas. Seek your vet's advice.

OLD AGE

Most small animals show very little signs of aging until a few months or weeks before the end of their life. Up to this time, they are usually alert and active, and enjoy their usual activities.

An older chipmunk may start to look a little grey, and may even become somewhat bald in places. This will not inconvenience it, but check that the skin at these sites does not become thickened or sore, as this may indicate mites.

The animal may become a little rheumaticky or arthritic and be reluctant to move much. As long as it seems to be enjoying life let it alone, but consult your vet if you think its condition is deteriorating.

Don't forget that, in the wild, a sick animal will be found and quickly killed by a predator. Nature has found a way of making sure it does not suffer for long. With our pets, we have to take the place of Nature, by asking the vet to put down a sick animal before it stops enjoying life altogether. Knowing that you are doing the right thing does not make it easier, but how you will cope with this situation is part of owning animals and is something you should consider before having a pet.

This cage has a wire floor. The faeces and urine can drop through which helps to keep the cage clean.

HIBERNATION

Chipmunks that are kept outside may hibernate, particularly if the weather is cold and damp, but those kept indoors or that have access to heated accommodation will not need to do this.

The pouches of this white chipmunk are bulging with food which it is taking back to its nest. If your chipmunks are going to hibernate, make sure they have extra food so that they can build up a good supply of fat.

Hibernating chipmunks will use their nest box, or they may burrow into the material on the base of the cage if it is suitable. You must make sure that the nest is not situated in a place where frost can reach it. Also, the chipmunks need to build up a fat supply in the months prior to hibernation, so you must give them a good diet during those months.

If you buy a new chipmunk and you think it has not got enough fat to take through a period of hibernation, keep it warm and do not let it hibernate.

It is unusual for chipmunks to hibernate all through the winter. Usually they disappear for a couple of days at a time during particularly nasty weather.

Although the Siberian chipmunk is the most common of the chipmunks kept in captivity, other species have been kept with varying degrees of success. All can be kept in the same way as the Siberian.

EUTAMIAS (WESTERN AMERICAN AND EUROPEAN CHIPMUNKS)

Various species of chipmunk are found in North America, Asia and parts of Europe. They all have black or brown back stripes separated by off-white or buff stripes.Their ranges often overlap, and they can be found from the plains to mountain tops. Although both habits and habitats differ from species to species, most *Eutamias* chipmunks seem to be more social and less shy than the Siberian.

This chipmunk is a colour variation called cinnamon. Breeders are finding more mutations in colour.

The Alpine Chipmunk *(Eutamias alpinus)* This species is yellowish-grey, and its side stripes are dark red or brown, not black, although the stripe down the centre of the back is black. The underneath of the tail is bright orange, the tail itself is 16–20cm (6.2–8in).

A white (left) and a normal (right) will happily share a cage together.

The Cliff Chipmunk *(Eutamias speciosus)* The body stripes on this medium-sized chipmunk are very indistinct and, in some cases, vanish altogether. However, the head stripes are very clear. The tail is bushy and a rusty red underneath. This chipmunk is approximately 19–27cm (7.5–10.5in) long.

The Least Chipmunk *(Eutamias minimus)* As its name suggests, this is one of the smallest of the chipmunks, growing only to about 16–22cm (6–8.5in) long. This species has a very wide range. The coat colour varies according to which part of the range the chipmunk comes from; it is more yellow with tan stripes in drier areas and brownish-grey with black side stripes in wetter places.

Whatever the species or colour, all chipmunks are lively agile animals
that will give you lots of pleasure.

The Long Eared Chipmunk *(Eutamias quadrimaculatus)* The distinguishing features of this chipmunk, as you might guess from its name, are the long ears with their white patch behind and dark strip below.

Merriam's Chipmunk *(Eutamias merriami)* This species has distinct white stomach fur. Generally it is a grey-brown colour, and the stripes are not sharply defined. The long tail is edged with buff or white hairs.

The Sonoma Chipmunk *(Eutamias sonomae)* This chipmunk grows to 22cm (8.5in) long. The stripes are not as distinct in this species as in some others. The underneath of the tail is reddish, as are the stripes on the head.

Townsend's Chipmunk *(Eutamias townsendii)* This larger species (up to 31cm/12in) is dark brown with grey-black and white stripes on its head and down the body. The tail is very distinctive, being long and bushy, black on top with lots of white-tipped hairs and reddish-brown bordered with black below. The ears also are very noticeable. The backs are dusky on the front half and grey on the back.

The Yellow Pine Chipmunk *(Eutamias amoenus)* This brightly-coloured chipmunk can grow up to 24cm (9.5in). Its colour ranges from tawny to a pinky-cinnamon. The top of the head is brown and the ears are blackish in front and off-white behind.

TAMIAS (EASTERN AMERICAN CHIPMUNK)

The Eastern American Chipmunk *(Tamias striatus)* lives in the eastern half of the United States and the southeast of Canada. It is more solitary than the Western American and Siberian species and can be very aggressive, even in the wild, so it is rarely seen in captivity. It is included in this section in case you ever have the opportunity to own one.

The Eastern American species do not form pairs during the breeding season and, for this reason and because of their aggressive nature, they should not be kept together. When the female is calling, introduce the male to her cage and remove him as soon as possible. If you leave the two together, you will probably have a dead male on your hands. It would also be wise to separate the babies as soon as they are weaned.

The Eastern American needs more space than the other two species, but does not need such a high cage as it is more of a ground dweller. The nest boxes can be sited lower down as well. Apart from this, diet, general care and health are very much the same as for the Siberian.

The chipmunk keeps a bright eye on the camera to make sure its treat is not taken away.

The tail of the white chipmunk appears to have less fur on it than other colours.

IN CONCLUSION

I hope that you have found this book helpful, and that you enjoy your chipmunk friends. Always remember that the chipmunks will have to rely on you for their food, housing, warmth and comfort. They are your responsibility. If you carry out your duties properly, you will be rewarded by having happy, healthy pets that will give you many hours of fun and companionship.

A happy female chipmunk.

Your First Series

Aquarium	185279052 0	YFK100
Budgerigar	185279051 2	YFK102
Canary	185279037 7	YFK103
Chipmunk	185279121 7	YFK508
Cockatiel	185279038 5	YFK104
Dwarf Hamster	185279122 5	YFK509
Fancy Rat	185279056 3	YFK501
Ferret	185279046 6	YFK105
Finch	185279049 0	YFK106
Gerbil	185279039 3	YFK107
Giant African Land Snail	185279057 1	YFK502
Goldfish	185279040 7	YFK108
Guinea Pig	185279041 5	YFK109
Hamster	185279042 3	YFK110
Kitten	185279055 5	YFK118
Koi	185279059 8	YFK504
Lizard	185279043 1	YFK111
Lovebird	185279045 8	YFK112
Millipede and Cockroach	185279082 2	YFK505
Mouse	185279048 2	YFK120
Parrot	185279044 X	YFK113
Pond	185279081 4	YFK506
Puppy	185279054 7	YFK119
Rabbit	185279050 4	YFK114
Snake	185279047 4	YFK115
Stick Insect	185279079 2	YFK507
Terrapin	185279058 X	YFK503
Tropical Fish	185279053 9	YFK116

Everything you need to know to start with
CHIPMUNKS

KINGDOM

YFK-508

ISBN 1852791217

9 781852 791216